HISPANIC LEADERS OF COURAGE



# SONIA SOTOMAYOR

EZRA E. KNOPP

PowerKiDS press

Published in 2026 by The Rosen Publishing Group, Inc.
2544 Clinton Street, Buffalo, NY 14224



First Edition

Editor: Theresa Emminizer
Book Design: Michael Flynn

Photo Credits: Cover, pp. 1, 5 https://commons.wikimedia.org/wiki/File:Sonia_Sotomayor_in_SCOTUS_robe.jpg; (series background) Sergei Mishchenko/Shutterstock.com; p. 7 https://commons.wikimedia.org/wiki/File:Sonia_Sotomayor_12_with_parents.jpg; p. 9 https://commons.wikimedia.org/wiki/File:Sonia_Sotomayor_13_age_six_or_seven.jpg; p. 11 https://commons.wikimedia.org/wiki/File:Sonia_Sotomayor_14_8th_grade_graduation.jpg; p. 13 Stacey Ilyse Photography/GM/Current Affairs/Alamy Stock Photo; p. 15 https://commons.wikimedia.org/wiki/File:Sonia_Sotomayor_(32372778021).jpg; p. 17 https://commons.wikimedia.org/wiki/File:SCOTUSJusticeSotomayorandObamaatReception.jpg; p. 19 https://commons.wikimedia.org/wiki/File:O%27Connor,_Sotomayor,_Ginsburg,_and_Kagan.jpg, p. 21 Photo Win1/Shutterstock.com.

Library of Congress Cataloging-in-Publication Data

Names: Knopp, Ezra E., author.
Title: Sonia Sotomayor / Ezra E. Knopp.
Description: Buffalo : PowerKids Press, 2025. | Series: Hispanic leaders of courage | Includes index.
Identifiers: LCCN 2024043409 (print) | LCCN 2024043410 (ebook) | ISBN 9781499451160 (library binding) | ISBN 9781499451153 (paperback) | ISBN 9781499451177 (ebook)
Subjects: LCSH: Sotomayor, Sonia, 1954–Juvenile literature. | Hispanic American judges–Biography–Juvenile literature. | Judges–United States–Biography–Juvenile literature. | United States. Supreme Court–Officials and employees–Biography–Juvenile literature.
Classification: LCC KF8745.S67 K56 2025 (print) | LCC KF8745.S67 (ebook) | DDC 347.73/2634 [B]–dc23/eng/20240917
LC record available at https://lccn.loc.gov/2024043409
LC ebook record available at https://lccn.loc.gov/2024043410

Manufactured in China

# CONTENTS

## Trailblazer

Sonia Sotomayor is the first Hispanic person, and third woman, to serve on the U.S. Supreme Court, the highest court in the country! From **humble** beginnings, Sonia worked hard to earn her education and place on the Supreme Court. Her strong leadership and careful decisions, or choices, have changed American history.

## Born in the Bronx

Sonia Sotomayor was born on June 25, 1954, in New York City. Her parents, Juan and Celina, were from Puerto Rico. Sonia also had a little brother named Juan. Sonia's mother was a nurse, and her father was a factory worker. The family lived in the Bronx.

## Growing Up

Sonia's family had little money and faced many problems. When she was seven years old, Sonia found out she had **diabetes**. When she was nine, Sonia's father died. Sonia found joy in stories. She loved to read Nancy Drew books and watch *Perry Mason*, a show about court cases.

# A Star Student

Sonia was a good student and did very well in high school. She was the top of her class and her grades were very good. Her hard work earned her a full **scholarship** to Princeton University. After Princeton, she went to Yale Law School to become a lawyer.

## Practicing Law

Sonia came back to New York to serve as an assistant **district attorney**. She spent five years in the courtroom, handling crime cases. In 1984, Sonia went to work at a law firm called Pavia & Harcourt. She later became a partner there.

## A Federal Judge

In 1991, Sonia was **nominated** to the U.S. District Court, Southern District of New York, by President George H.W. Bush. In this role, she ruled on 450 cases, one of which ended a Major League Baseball **strike**. Sonia then served as a judge on another important U.S. court until 2009.

## Supreme Court Justice

During her time as a federal judge, Sonia also taught at Columbia Law School and New York University Law School. On May 26, 2009, she was nominated as an Associate Justice of the Supreme Court by President Barack Obama. On August 8, 2009, Sonia Sotomayor became the first Latina on the Supreme Court!

## Important Decisions

Over her many years as a federal judge and Supreme Court Justice, Sonia heard thousands of cases. Her rulings on these cases helped shape American life and law. Sonia helped **legalize** same-sex marriage. She also voted to uphold the Affordable Care Act, to help Americans get health care without spending too much.

## Making History

Sonia Sotomayor's hard work and skill as a lawyer took her to the most powerful court in the land. Known for her careful questioning and thoughtful choices, her rulings have changed American history. As a Hispanic leader, Sonia's life and work continues to move young people to follow their dreams.

# Sonia Steps Up

## June 25th, 1954

Sonia is born in New York City.

## November 1991

President George H.W. Bush nominates Sonia to the U.S. District Court for the Southern District of New York.

## June 1997

President Bill Clinton nominates Sonia to the U.S. Court of Appeals for the Second Circuit.

## May 26, 2009

President Barack Obama nominates Sonia as an Associate Justice of the Supreme Court.

## August 8, 2009

Sonia becomes the first Latina on the U.S. Supreme Court.

## 2013

Sonia's book, *My Beloved World*, comes out.

# GLOSSARY

**diabetes:** An illness of the body's ability to make or respond to the hormone insulin.

**district attorney:** A government lawyer who makes cases against people who do crimes.

**humble:** Modest or not costly.

**nominated:** Appointed or proposed for appointment to an office or place.

**scholarship:** Money given to a student to help pay for further schooling.

**strike:** When workers refuse to work until certain conditions are met.

# FOR MORE INFORMATION

## BOOKS

Gaston, Stephanie. *Sonia Sotomayor.* New York, NY: Crabtree Publishing Company, 2023.

Romo Edelman, Claudia, and Nathalie Alonso. *Sonia Sotomayor.* New York, NY: Roaring Brook Press, 2023.

## WEBSITES

**National Museum of the American Latino**
*latino.si.edu/exhibitions/presente/shaping-nation/sonia-sotomayor*
Discover how Sotomayor broke boundaries as a Latina leader in American government.

**Supreme Court Historical Society**
*supremecourthistory.org/supreme-court-justices/associate-justice-sonia-sotomayor/*
Find out more about Sonia Sotomayor's work on the Supreme Court.

Publisher's note to educators and parents: Our editors have carefully reviewed these websites to ensure that they are suitable for students. Many websites change frequently, however, and we cannot guarantee that a site's future contents will continue to meet our high standards of quality and educational value. Be advised that students should be closely supervised whenever they access the internet.

# INDEX